Babe Ruth

SADDLEBACK
EDUCATIONAL PUBLISHING

Saddleback's Graphic Biographies

SADDLEBACK
EDUCATIONAL PUBLISHING
www.sdlback.com

ISBN-13: 978-1-59905-215-1
ISBN-10: 1-59905-215-6
eBook: 978-1-60291-578-7

Printed in Malaysia

21 20 19 18 17   8 9 10 11 12

BABE RUTH

The year was 1914. It was the Baltimore Orioles' first game in spring training camp. A nineteen-year-old rookie was at bat. He swung, the ball went up, and up, and out over the fence.

That's the longest ball ever hit at this field! Who is that guy?

Some rookie named Ruth!

It was Babe Ruth's first game as a professional player.

And the next day ...

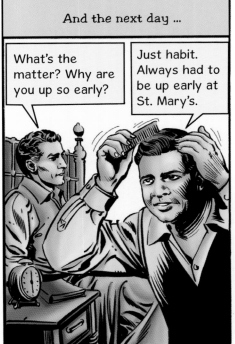

What's the matter? Why are you up so early?

Just habit. Always had to be up early at St. Mary's.

He left the hotel.

Which way's the railroad station?

Right down that-a-way, sir!

At the station ...

All right if I hang around for a while?

Sure. You catching a train?

FAYETTEVILLE STATION

Oh, no. I just want to watch 'em. I never saw trains before.

FAY STA

Boy! That's the greatest! All that power!

FAYETTEVILLE STATION

He was back at the hotel for breakfast.

Is it really true? We order what we want and the ball club pays for it?

Yes—and I think they're going to lose money on you!

Babe made friends with boys who hung around the practice field.

Say, will you show me how to pitch?

You bet!

You hold the ball like this ...

Then the windup ...

Then you throw and follow through!

Now will you let me ride your bike?

Sure, take mine!

No! Mine!

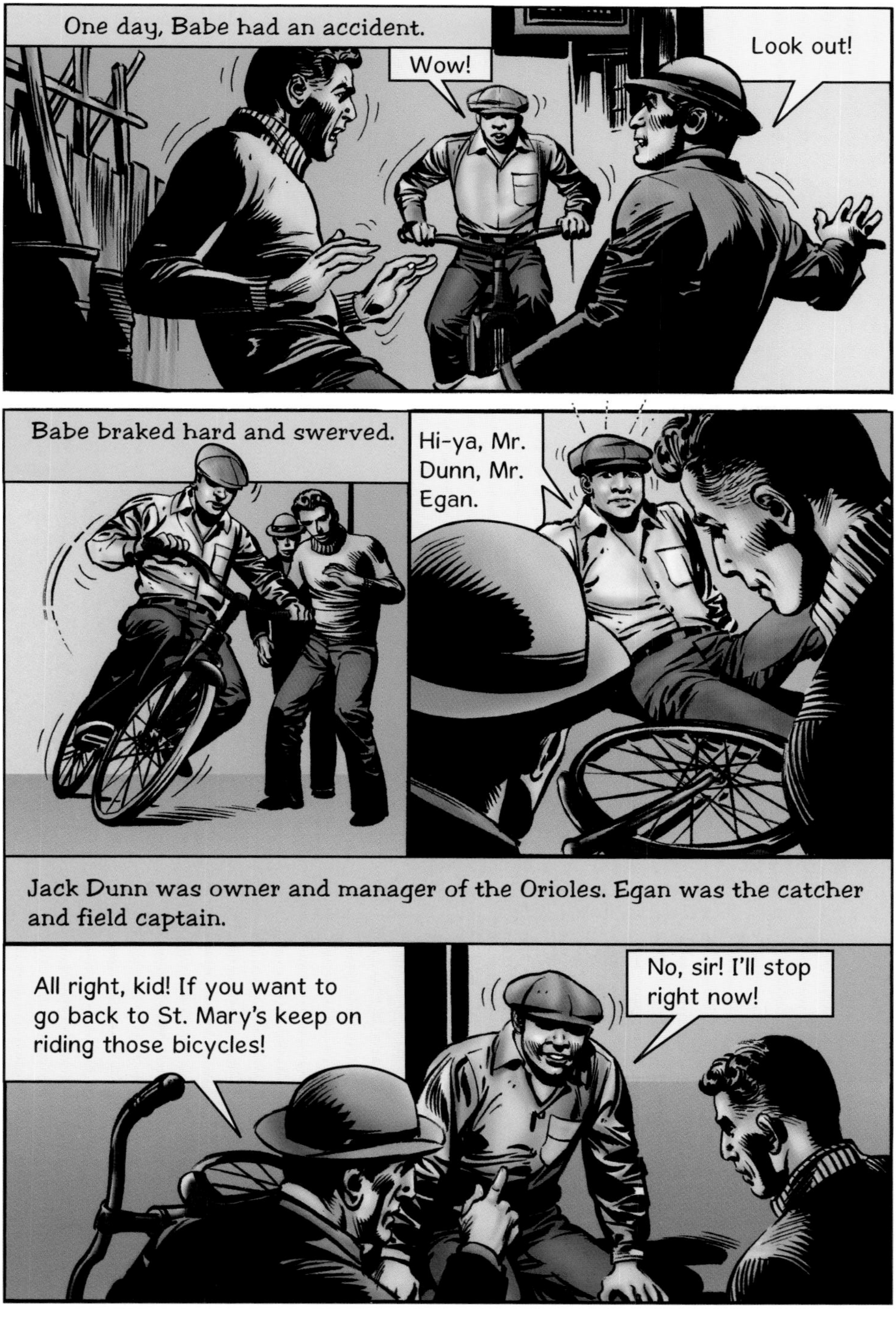
One day, Babe had an accident.
Wow!
Look out!
Babe braked hard and swerved.
Hi-ya, Mr. Dunn, Mr. Egan.
Jack Dunn was owner and manager of the Orioles. Egan was the catcher and field captain.
All right, kid! If you want to go back to St. Mary's keep on riding those bicycles!
No, sir! I'll stop right now!

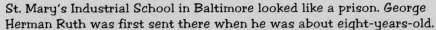

St. Mary's Industrial School in Baltimore looked like a prison. George Herman Ruth was first sent there when he was about eight-years-old.

Now George, I see you're here because you are "incorrigible." Do you know what that means?

No.

It means that you wouldn't obey the rules. Here, I am in charge of making people obey.

Gosh.

I'd think anybody'd have to obey *you!*

Ha-ha! Well, see that you do! Now come out and let's play some baseball.

Hit some for us, Brother Matthias.

Hit one over the fence!

I never saw anybody swing at a ball like that before!

But St. Mary's was not all baseball.

You'll sleep here, George. We go to bed at eight o'clock.

You get up at 6 o'clock and wash, dress, attend mass, eat breakfast, and be in your school classroom at 7:30 a.m.

Wow!

After lunch each day, the boys worked in a shop to learn a trade.

This is George Ruth. He's to work here in the shirt factory.

All right, George. We'll teach you to put collars on shirts.

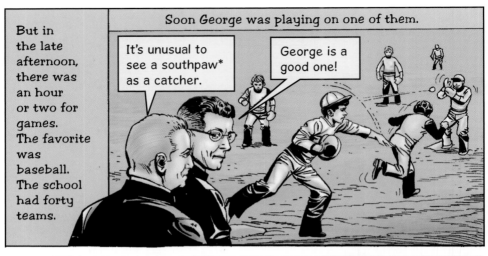

But in the late afternoon, there was an hour or two for games. The favorite was baseball. The school had forty teams.

Soon *George* was playing on one of them.

It's unusual to see a southpaw* as a catcher.

George is a good one!

Later ...

George, you're big for your age, and a good player. We'll put you on an older boys' team.

That'll be swell!

Then there was another change.

We need a pitcher on our star team. Why don't you try it?

Gosh! I don't know how to pitch!

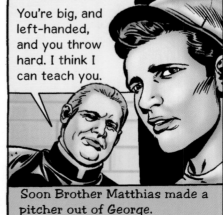

You're big, and left-handed, and you throw hard. I think I can teach you.

Soon Brother Matthias made a pitcher out of *George*.

* in sports, a player who throws with the left hand

When George was nineteen, there was a game between St. Mary's star team and Mount St. Joseph's. It was a holiday and a big event.

Yaaaaay! We won! Ruth pitched a shut-out! Twenty-two strike-outs! What pitchin'!

Soon afterward, George was called into the office.

George, this is Mr. Dunn, owner of the Oriole baseball team.

You did some nice pitching out there!

Uh, th-thanks.

Mr. Dunn would like you to play for his team next season as a professional.

Me, a baseball pro, oh, gosh!

It's the international league, the closest thing to the majors, with a chance to move up.

It's a great chance, George. Mr. Dunn will pay you $600 for the year. He will become your guardian until you are 21.

Oh, yes!

Good! We'll leave soon for spring training camp in North Carolina.

But do you think I can make it out there?

You'll make it, George!

Soon George left St. Mary's. He took his first train ride, to Fayettesville, and followed Jack Dunn out onto the field.

Who is that?

Just Dunnie, with his newest babe.

"Babe" was a common baseball word for rookies. But from then on, George Ruth was known as "Babe." It suited him.

He had spent most of his life at St. Mary's. He didn't know about trains or hotels or bicycles or money. But he knew about baseball.

In his first game, he hit the ball farther than any had ever seen in that park before or since.

The Orioles went on the road. He pitched his first complete game against the best team in baseball, the Philadelphia Athletics.

That kid's the most promising youngster I've ever seen!

The regular season began.

During training, the club paid your expenses. Now you get a salary, $50 every two weeks.

Thanks! I never had more than five dollars at once before!

See that you take care of it!

Babe hurried to a shop.

I want the best you've got—up to $50.

Certainly, sir!

And he roared off on a new red motorcycle.

He kept playing well. In May ...

I'm doubling your salary, Babe.

And in June ...

Babe, I'm giving you another raise to $180.

Thanks, Mr. Dunn!

But things were not going well for Dunn.

I've given Baltimore a winning team and the people don't turn out to see us! I am going broke. I have to trade some players.

On Thursday, July 10, 1914, Dunn made on announcement.

Gentlemen, I have traded Ruth, Shore, and Eagan to the Boston Red Sox.

Saturday morning Babe and the others reached Boston.

First thing, let's check into a hotel.

And second thing, let's eat breakfast.

They went to a nearby coffee shop.

Hello beautiful! Bring me a double order of bacon and eggs!

You must be hungry!

Soon she and Babe were going out together.

They're sending me to the Providence farm team. They have a good chance of winning their pennant race, but they need a pitcher.

Oh, Babe! I'll miss you!

You won't have a chance to. It's only forty miles away!

With Babe's help, the Providence Grays were the winners in the International League. Babe finished the season with a total of 28 wins and 9 losses.

But the season was ending.

I'll be in Baltimore for the winter. It may be April before I see you again!

Look, hon, how about you and me getting married?

Oh, gosh! I don't know. Yes!

They were married at St. Paul's Catholic Church, near Baltimore.

Babe was only twenty-years-old, but he had a job in the major leagues and a good salary. In a few months, he had come a long way.

On May 5, 1915, Babe pitched against the New York Yankees at the Polo Grounds in New York. He came to bat in the third inning.

A home run into the upper right stands! Wow!

And hit by a left-handed pitcher!

This was Babe's first major league home run.

Babe pitched a 13-inning game and lost 4-3.

We lost!

Just the same, you did a good job! I'm putting you in the regular pitching rotation.

His fourth and last home run of the season came in July in St Louis.

Look at that! Clear outa the ballpark!

Hey! It busted a plate glass window in a store!

It was the longest ball ever hit in the St. Louis park. Babe also hit two doubles and a single and pitched a complete game to win 4-3.

The Red Sox won the pennant, but Babe did not get in the World Series.

I can do it. Just give me a chance!

I know it, Babe, but I'm going with right-handed pitching as long as it works.

It worked. The Red Sox were World Champions. And Babe got a check as a member of the winning team.

That's not bad, $3,780.25! That's more than my whole salary! Let's throw a party!

In 1916 Babe had a great season. The fans loved him.

What a guy! Twenty-three wins and nine shutouts.

And he hit three home runs in one game!

Once again, the Red Sox were world champions. Babe pitched a 14-inning game—the longest ever played in a World Series game.

In 1918 the Red Sox had a new manager, Ed Barrow.

You're a star pitcher, Babe, but you're also a great hitter. And you like to hit.

Suppose you play the outfield on the days you don't pitch. That way we can use you every day instead of every fourth day.

I think I will hit better if I can play every day.

For the next three days, Babe Ruth played first-base or outfielder. On the 4th day, he pitched ten innings.

This guy's the best! Three home runs in three days, and his batting average is up to 484.

And the fans love it!

That season, Babe hit eleven home runs. It was the beginning of a new era in baseball.

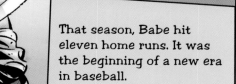

A big change was on the way for Babe. In early 1920, he met the Yankee manager, Miller Huggins.

Hello, Babe. Can I talk to you?

Sure. Have I been traded to the Yankees?

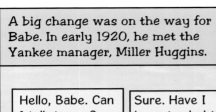

That's right, in a deal worth $450,000 to the Red Sox owner. The Yankees really want you!

And we'll double your salary to $20,000 a year.

Well, I like Boston, but I'll play as hard for the Yankees as I did for the Red Sox!

When the news was announced, the Boston fans were angry.

I'll never forgive Frazee for this!

I figure the Red Sox are ruined!

BABE GOES TO YANKEES

And when Babe reported to the Yankees to take the train for spring training camp, he was mobbed by happy New York fans.

Yaaaaay, Babe!

How many home runs next season, Babe?

He started the season in a slump. But on May 1st he hit his first home run.

Come on, big boy!

Now Babe was famous all over the country. And on road trips, there were problems.

You're Babe Ruth's roommate. Tell us what he's like.

I don't room with Baby Ruth. I room with his suitcase.

At night, Babe would rather go to parties than go to bed.

You can't stay out all night and break all the training rules and still play good baseball. I'm going to fine you!

Sometimes the Babe was fined, even suspended. But he never really learned to follow the rules.

With Babe as its star, the Yankee team drew such crowds it was able to build a new home. Yankee Stadium opened April 18, 1923.

It's the greatest place I ever saw!

The baseball writers are calling it "The House that Ruth Built."

Babe and Helen had separated. In 1923 he met Claire Hodgson and fell in love.

In 1929 Helen died. A few months later the Babe and Claire were married.

I want to marry you, Claire. But Helen and I are Catholic and don't believe in divorce.

I understand. We'll be good friends anyway.

Afterward, they talked to reporters.

Where are you going on your honeymoon?

We're not going on a honeymoon. We're going to work and win another pennant!

The next day was spring training. The new Mrs. Babe Ruth went to the game.

Babe hit a home run and blew a kiss to Claire as he rounded third base.

Claire had a daughter, Julia, by another marriage. Babe had an adopted daughter, Dorothy. Now the families were united.

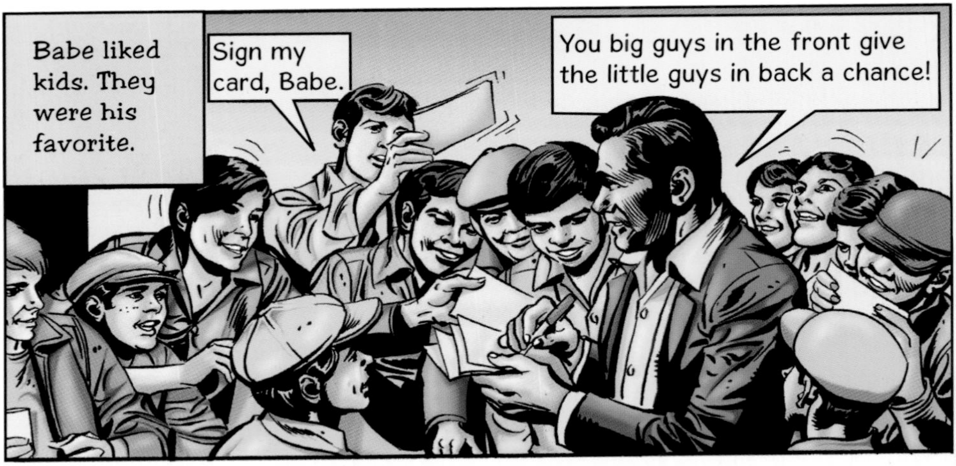
Babe liked kids. They were his favorite.
Sign my card, Babe.
You big guys in the front give the little guys in back a chance!

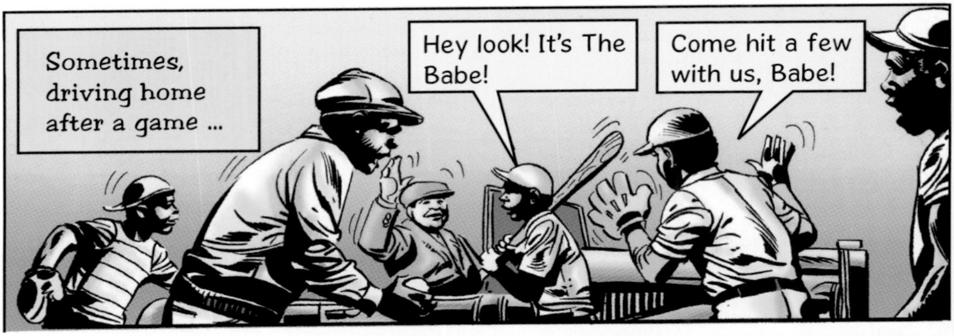
Sometimes, driving home after a game ...
Hey look! It's The Babe!
Come hit a few with us, Babe!

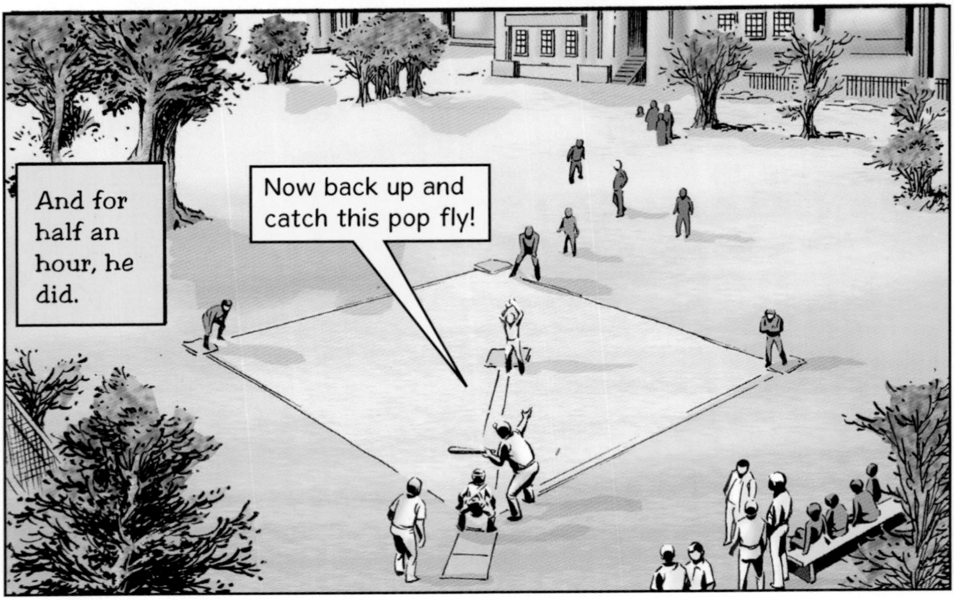
And for half an hour, he did.
Now back up and catch this pop fly!

There were kids in hospitals too. He visited them all over the country.

Okay, you hold the bat like this. When you're a little stronger, you can swing it!

From 1926 through 1932, Babe Ruth averaged 50 home runs a year, batted .354, and played in seven Yankee World Series.

Another Yankee series!

And that Babe! Can you believe he's 37-years-old?

He held or shared 61 baseball records. Twenty-eight were World Series records. And his lifetime home run record—714—would not be broken for forty years!

He stopped playing in 1935. But 12 years later he had not been forgotten.

Did you see this? Babe Ruth's in the hospital!

Gosh! I wish I could see him play baseball!

Letters for Babe Ruth. There's more outside!

Thirty thousand letters arrived. And when he left, it took the police to get him to his car.

Good luck, Babe!

Get well quick!

And then ...

The commissioner of baseball has declared Sunday, April 27th as Babe Ruth Day—all over the major leagues!

In New York too!

And they want me to come to Yankee Stadium.

Sixty thousand other people came!

And now ladies and gentlemen, the Babe!

Thank you very much, ladies and gentlemen. This game of ours comes up from the youth, the boys ...

There's been so many lovely things said about me. I'm glad I had the opportunity to thank everybody. Thank you!

On August 16, 1948, the Babe died. His body was moved to "The House that Ruth Built" to lie in state for two days at the Yankee Stadium rotunda.

People came—71,000 of them—to say goodbye. On the day of the funeral, 80,000 stood on Fifth Avenue to watch as his coffin passed.

THE END